WOMEN PILOTS
OF WORLD WAR II

Lisa L. Owens

Lerner Publications ◆ Minneapolis

Content consultant: Eric Juhnke, Professor of History,
Briar Cliff University

Lerner Publications Company
An imprint of Lerner Publishing Group, Inc.
241 First Avenue North
Minneapolis, MN 55401 USA

For reading levels and more information, look up this title at
www.lernerbooks.com.

Main body text set in Aptifer Slab LT Pro Regular.
Typeface provided by Linotype AG.

Library of Congress Cataloging-in-Publication Data

Names: Owens, L. L., author.
Title: Women pilots of World War II / Lisa L. Owens.
Description: Minneapolis : Lerner Publications, 2018. | Series: Heroes
   of World War II | Includes bibliographical references and index. |
   Audience: Grades 4–6.
Identifiers: LCCN 2017044067 (print) | LCCN 2017050382 (ebook) |
   ISBN 9781541521605 (eb pdf) | ISBN 9781541521537 (lb : alk. paper)
Subjects: LCSH: Women Airforce Service Pilots (U.S.)—Juvenile
   literature. | Women air pilots—United States—Juvenile literature. |
   Air pilots, Military—United States—Juvenile literature. | World
   War, 1939–1945—Aerial operations, American—Juvenile literature. |
   World War, 1939–1945—Participation, Female—Juvenile literature.
Classification: LCC D790.5 (ebook) | LCC D790.5 .O94 2018 (print) | DDC
   940.54/4973082—dc23

LC record available at https://lccn.loc.gov/2017044067

Manufactured in the United States of America
2-52352-34647-6/10/2022

CONTENTS

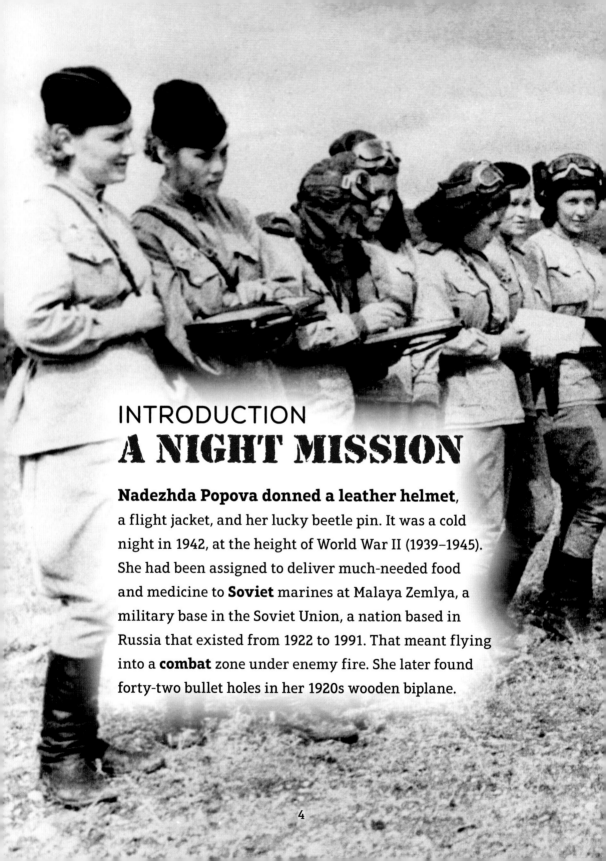

INTRODUCTION
A NIGHT MISSION

Nadezhda Popova donned a leather helmet, a flight jacket, and her lucky beetle pin. It was a cold night in 1942, at the height of World War II (1939–1945). She had been assigned to deliver much-needed food and medicine to **Soviet** marines at Malaya Zemlya, a military base in the Soviet Union, a nation based in Russia that existed from 1922 to 1991. That meant flying into a **combat** zone under enemy fire. She later found forty-two bullet holes in her 1920s wooden biplane.

Women pilots of the Night Bomber Regiment receive orders for a mission in 1944.

The mission was for the Soviet Union's 588th Night Bomber Regiment, an air force unit made up of only women. When the war started in 1939, the Soviets didn't allow women in combat. But by October 1941, the Soviet Air Force needed more pilots. They were willing to begin training women for the job.

Nadezhda Popova completed her first solo flight when she was sixteen years old. She later went to pilot school and became a flight instructor.

Popova eagerly joined her unit at the age of nineteen. Each night she flew missions to bomb German military bases. Once she completed eighteen bombings in one night. She said she had to "sail through a wall of enemy fire" almost every time. In all, Popova carried out 852 missions.

The Soviet Union was the only **Allied** country to send women pilots into combat during World War II. But many other women pilots served the Allied nations. They all played an important role in serving their countries and helping the Allies win the war.

Two members of the Night Bomber Regiment

CHAPTER 1
WOMEN PILOTS ON THE RISE

When Pauline Gower, a British nineteen-year-old, told her parents she wanted to be a pilot, they refused to support her. At the time, it was uncommon for women to be pilots, and many people believed women should not fly planes. They thought women were not strong or calm enough to be pilots.

Gower waves from her plane before a flight in 1940.

But Gower was determined. She taught violin lessons to earn money, and she began taking flying lessons. She quickly earned her pilot's license, and within two years, she had her own airplane and her own flying business.

FINDING THE ATA GIRLS

When World War II broke out in 1939, Britain knew it would not have enough pilots to support the war effort. Sir Gerard John Regis Leo d'Erlanger, director of British

Sir Gerard John Regis Leo d'Erlanger

Airways, wrote to the Air Ministry and suggested that Royal Air Force (RAF) pilots could do their job better in wartime if **civilian** pilots transported airplanes from factories to military bases. The Air Ministry put d'Erlanger in charge of forming an organization of civilian pilots, called the Air Transport Auxiliary (ATA). Within one month of the start of the war, d'Erlanger had selected thirty men to serve in the ATA.

Two months later, the ATA began **recruiting** women. Many in Britain were still against the idea of women working as pilots. C. G. Grey, the editor of *Aeroplane* magazine, wrote, "There are millions of women in

A group of ATA women
wearing flight gear in 1940

Britain recruited women to the Women's Auxiliary Air Force (*pictured*). These women were not pilots. Instead, they worked as mechanics, electricians, code breakers, and in many other roles.

the country who could do useful jobs in war. But the trouble is that so many of them insist on wanting to do jobs which they are quite incapable of doing."

But Pauline Gower, by this time a well-known pilot, fought in favor of the ATA recruiting women. The ATA soon brought her on to form a women's section of the group. The program began with just eight female pilots.

Jackie Cochran began flying in 1932. After the war, she became the first woman to fly faster than the speed of sound.

A US PILOT PROGRAM

Meanwhile, in the United States, Jacqueline (Jackie) Cochran, an air-racing champion, was hatching her own plans. She thought the US military should recruit women pilots. In 1939 Cochran presented her ideas to Eleanor Roosevelt, who suggested she speak with Army Air Corps commander General H. H. Arnold. He rejected her ideas. But by 1941, the United States was watching the war in Europe closely. Arnold asked Cochran to take twenty-five women pilots to England to study the ATA. If the United States started a program for women pilots, he would consult with her.

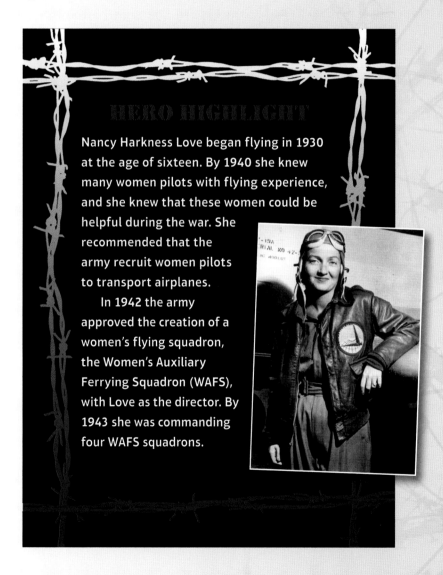

HERO HIGHLIGHT

Nancy Harkness Love began flying in 1930 at the age of sixteen. By 1940 she knew many women pilots with flying experience, and she knew that these women could be helpful during the war. She recommended that the army recruit women pilots to transport airplanes.

In 1942 the army approved the creation of a women's flying squadron, the Women's Auxiliary Ferrying Squadron (WAFS), with Love as the director. By 1943 she was commanding four WAFS squadrons.

CHAPTER 2
PILOT TRAINING

In England, Cochran flew under Gower and learned how
to run a piloting program to fit US military needs. But
in 1942, she returned to the United States and found
out that the military had already started a program for
women pilots—without consulting her. Cochran quickly
met with Arnold. She convinced him to start a second
program, the Women's Flying Training Detachment
(WFTD), with Cochran in charge.

**Members of WFTD on
their way to class**

Women pilots prepare for a training flight at Avenger Field in 1944.

AVENGER FIELD

In 1943 the WAFS and WFTD combined to form the Women Airforce Service Pilots (WASP), directed by Cochran. More than twenty-five thousand women applied to join. Only about eighteen hundred made the cut. The women began training at Avenger Field in Sweetwater, Texas. Pilots underwent six months of flight training and ground school, including classes in math, physics, weather, and navigation. They practiced flying in daylight and at night. They had to be ready to handle any challenges that might happen during flight.

Flights by US Women Pilots during WWII

WASPS AT WORK

Just 1,074 women graduated from the difficult training program. Then they went to military bases all over the country. In addition to flying planes from factories to military bases, they also tested planes and towed targets that male soldiers used to practice shooting.

Deanie Parrish towed targets at Tyndall Air Force Base in Florida. "These [soldiers] were 'green gunners,'" she said, "which means they were learning and some couldn't shoot as straight as others." The job was especially dangerous because she flew a B-26 Martin Marauder. The plane was nicknamed Flying Coffin because many pilots felt it was too dangerous to fly. But Parrish mastered the plane, and it soon became her favorite.

STEM HIGHLIGHT

Pilots had to be able to fly—and land—even if it was too dark or cloudy to see where they were going. The Link flight **simulator** helped train them for this possibility. The device resembled a small plane's cockpit. Pilots learned to calculate their location and route using only the instrument panel, maps, and radio signals. Later, they used the same skills during real flights.

CHAPTER 3
THE GOOD FIGHT

Although most women pilots never engaged in battle, they were often in danger during their flights. They flew all the same planes that male military pilots flew. Planes and equipment could malfunction, and weather could be unpredictable.

WASPs carry their flight gear at an army base in Delaware.

A US pilot prepares to climb into her plane in 1943.

SECOND-CLASS EQUIPMENT

Margaret Phelan Taylor was in the air somewhere between Arizona and California when she noticed smoke in her cockpit. She knew she should bail out of the plane if anything went wrong during a flight. But her parachute was much too large for her, and it could be dangerous for her to bail out with a parachute that didn't fit. So she decided to stay in the plane until she saw flames. Luckily, the problem turned out to be a burned-out instrument.

Women pilots in the Soviet Union's 125th Guards Bomber Regiment were often too short to comfortably fly their planes, and male pilots did not trust the women's strength and skills.

Soviet pilots also struggled with equipment that did not fit properly. They wore uniforms and boots passed down from male pilots. Some women stuffed strips of cloth into their boots to make them fit. The women also flew in old, wooden planes without radios or parachutes. But the pilots understood the dangers of combat and were honored to serve their country. Pilot

Katya Budanova felt that if anything happened to her, she and her trusty plane would both be considered heroes.

A WORTHY SACRIFICE

British Argentine ATA pilot Maureen Dunlop wanted women to be allowed in combat. "I thought it was the

STEM HIGHLIGHT

WASPs performed test flights on the Boeing B-29 Superfortress bomber introduced during World War II. The B-29 was one of the first military aircrafts with **pressurized** crew areas. This allowed the flight crew to breathe safely at higher **altitudes**. Otherwise, they'd have needed bulky oxygen masks that restricted their movement.

Maureen Dunlop poses for a photo following a flight in 1944.

only fair thing," she said. "Why should only men be killed?"

Like the ATA pilots, WASPs did not fly in combat. But many WASPs shared Dunlop's views. Pilot Charlyne Creger said, "It was a rare group at a rare time that had something to offer and offered it. Even if it meant they were offering their lives. It was that important." In all, fifteen ATA women, thirty-eight WASPS, and thirty members of the 588th Night Bomber Regiment died while serving their countries.

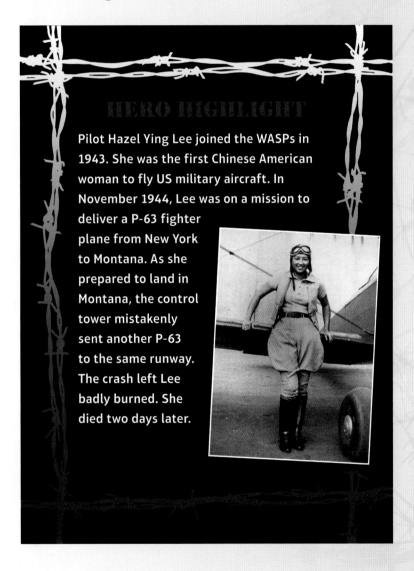

HERO HIGHLIGHT

Pilot Hazel Ying Lee joined the WASPs in 1943. She was the first Chinese American woman to fly US military aircraft. In November 1944, Lee was on a mission to deliver a P-63 fighter plane from New York to Montana. As she prepared to land in Montana, the control tower mistakenly sent another P-63 to the same runway. The crash left Lee badly burned. She died two days later.

CHAPTER 4
A LASTING LEGACY

At the war's end, many women pilots continued flying as instructors or professional racers—or just for fun. Some never flew again. But they all had a strong sense of pride in their service. Unlike their male counterparts, however, women pilots did not immediately gain recognition for their service during the war.

WASP Helen Snapp flies a mission in Georgia in 1944. She gave up flying after the war and went to work for the US Post Office. Snapp died in 2013.

SEEKING STATUS

WASPs did not have official military status. They were not granted military honors, and those who died in service did not receive military funerals. Near the end of the war, Jackie Cochran and General Arnold tried to get the WASPs official military status. However, Congress voted against the change. The WASP program disbanded in 1944.

WASP program records were not released until decades later. In 1977 Congress voted to give WASPs **veteran** status. They received the Congressional Gold Medal in March 2010, sixty-five years after the war. The medal honors civilians for achievements that contribute to the security and prosperity of the United States.

Deanie Parrish accepts the Congressional Gold Medal for her fellow WASPs in 2010.

The ATA disbanded in September 1945 as World War II ended. Its female members had achieved equal pay with men during the war, but they still waited decades for recognition. The prime minister of Britain presented Veterans Badges to surviving women pilots of the ATA in 2008.

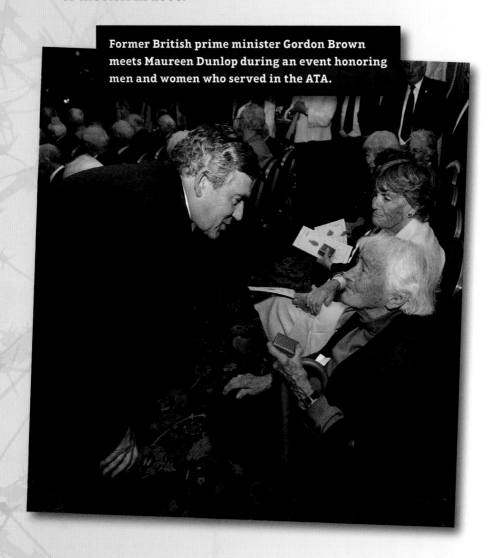

Former British prime minister Gordon Brown meets Maureen Dunlop during an event honoring men and women who served in the ATA.

Many Soviet women also received medals and awards for their service. Twenty-four members of the 588th Night Bomber Regiment received Hero of the Soviet Union stars, the highest award for service to the country.

Despite waiting years for official recognition, the women pilots of World War II accomplished what many of them set out to do: they served their countries, and they proved that women could fly in military roles. Male pilots often looked down on the women pilots. Some refused to fly or train with them. But in his speech to the last WASP graduates in 1944, General Arnold said, "You and more than 900 of your sisters have shown that you can fly wingtip to wingtip with your brothers. If ever there was any doubt in anyone's mind that women can be skillful pilots, the WASP have dispelled that doubt."

TIMELINE

September 1939	Germany invades Poland, marking the beginning of World War II in Europe. Britain forms the Air Transport Auxiliary (ATA) with Pauline Gower in charge of the women's ATA.
June 1941	Jackie Cochran goes to England to observe the Women's ATA.
October 1941	The Soviet Air Force forms three units of women pilots.
December 1941	The United States enters the war after Japan attacks Pearl Harbor.
April 1942	The first Soviet all-female aviation unit flies in a combat mission.
September 1942	The Women's Auxiliary Ferrying Squadron (WAFS) begins flying under Nancy Harkness Love's command.
August 1943	WAFS merges with the Women's Flying Training Detachment (WFTD) to form the Women Airforce Service Pilots (WASP), under Jackie Cochran's command.
December 1944	WASP disbands.

September 1945	World War II ends in an Allied victory. ATA disbands.
February 2008	Surviving women pilots of the ATA receive Veterans Badges.
March 2010	WASPs receive the Congressional Gold Medal.

Source Notes

6 Douglas Martin, "Nadezhda Popova, WWII 'Night Witch,' Dies at 91," *New York Times*, July 14, 2013, http://www.nytimes.com/2013/07/15/world/europe/nadezhda-popova-ww-ii-night-witch-dies-at-91.html?mcubz=0.

10–11 "A Brief History of the Air Transport Auxiliary," British Air Transport Auxiliary, accessed October 10, 2017, http://www.airtransportaux.com/history.html.

17 Chrissy Cuttita, "WASP Shares Her World War II Experiences," U.S. Air Force, March 30, 2006, http://www.af.mil/News/Features/Display/Article/143661/wasp-shares-her-world-war-ii-experiences.

21–22 Anne Keleny, "Maureen Dunlop: Pilot for the Air Transport Auxiliary Who Made the Cover of Picture Post," *Independent* (London), June 10, 2012, http://www.independent.co.uk/news/obituaries/maureen-dunlop-pilot-for-the-air-transport-auxiliary-who-made-the-cover-of-picture-post-7834571.html.

22–23 "Video Projects," Wings across America, accessed October 18, 2017, http://www.wingsacrossamerica.org/videos.html.

27 Susana J. Kelly, "WASPs: The World War II Women Who Flew," Wings across America, March 1998, http://www.wingsacrossamerica.us/wasp/resources/kelly.html#27.

Glossary

Allied: nations including the United States, Britain, and the Soviet Union that fought against Germany and other Axis powers during World War II

altitudes: heights above sea level

civilian: people who aren't members of the military

combat: active fighting in war

pressurized: increased air pressure in an enclosed space

recruiting: seeking people to join a group, organization, or military unit

simulator: a device that helps the operator train in conditions similar to the real situation

Soviet: relating to the Soviet Union, a nation based in Russia that existed from 1922 to 1991

veteran: someone who has served in the military

FURTHER INFORMATION

Doeden, Matt. *Tuskegee Airmen*. Minneapolis: Lerner Publications, 2019.

Ducksters: US Women of WWII
http://www.ducksters.com/history/world_war_ii/us_women_in_ww2.php

Garstecki, Julia. *WASPs*. Mankato, MN: Black Rabbit Books, 2017.

National WASP WWII Museum
http://waspmuseum.org/

Sherman, Jill. *Eyewitness to the Role of Women in World War II*. Mankato, MN: Child's World, 2016.

Women in Aviation: The Women's Section of the Air Transport Auxiliary
https://www.wai.org/pioneers/2008/womens-section-air -transport-auxiliary

Index

Photo Acknowledgments

The images in this book are used with the permission of: © iStockphoto.
com/akinshin (barbed wire background); Sovfoto/UIG/Getty Images, pp. 4–5,
29 (left); AF Fotografie/Alamy Stock Photo, p. 6; TASS/Getty Images, p. 7;
Imperial War Museums/Wikimedia Commons (public domain), p. 8; Mark
Kauffman/The LIFE Picture Collection/Getty Images, p. 9; Popperfoto/Getty
Images, p. 10; Planet News Archive/SSPL/Getty Images, p. 11; Bettmann/
Getty Images, pp. 12, 18; © U.S. Air Force/Courtesy of Woman's Collection,
Texas Woman's University, p. 13; Peter Stackpole/The LIFE Picture Collection/
Getty Images, p. 14; United States Army Air Forces/Wikimedia Commons
(public domain), p. 15; © Laura Westlund/Independent Picture Service, p. 16;
Wikimedia Commons (public domain), p. 17; Peter Stackpole/Life Magazine/
Time & Life Pictures/Getty Images, p. 19; AFP PHOTO/RIA NOVOSTI/Getty
Images, p. 20; © U.S. Air Force, pp. 21, 24, 28; Leonard McCombe/Picture Post/
Hulton Archive/Getty Images, p. 22; U.S. Air Force/Wikimedia Commons
(public domain), p. 23; © U.S. Air Force photo by Staff Sgt. J. G. Buzanowski,
p. 25; Carl Court/PA Images/Getty Images, p. 26; Sovfoto/UIG/Getty Images,
p. 29 (left); Popperfoto/Getty Images, p. 29 (right).

Front cover: PhotoQuest/Getty Images (women); © iStockphoto.com/
akinshin (barbed wire background); © iStockphoto.com/ElementalImaging
(camouflage background); © iStockphoto.com/MillefloreImages (flag
background).